MyPlate and Healthy Eating

Healthy Snacks, Healthy You!

BY SALLY LEE

ILLUSTRATED BY GARY SWIFT

Consultant: Amy Lusk, MS, RD, LD
Registered Dietitian
Nationwide Children's Hospital, Columbus, Ohio

CAPSTONE PRESS
a capstone imprint

First Graphics are published by Capstone Press,
151 Good Counsel Drive, P.O. Box 669, Mankato, Minnesota 56002.
www.capstonepub.com

 Books published by Capstone Press are manufactured with paper
containing at least 10 percent post-consumer waste.

Library of Congress Cataloging-in-Publication Data
Lee, Sally.
  Healthy snacks, healthy you! / by Sally Lee ; illustrated by Gary Swift.
    p. cm.—(First graphics. MyPlate and healthy eating)
  Summary: "Simple text and illustrations present MyPlate and examples of
healthy snack choices"—Provided by publisher.
  Includes bibliographical references and index.
  ISBN 978-1-4296-6093-8 (library binding)
  ISBN 978-1-4296-7162-0 (paperback)
  1. Snack foods—Juvenile literature. 2. Nutrition—Juvenile literature.
I. Swift, Gary, ill. II. Title.
  TX740.L37 2012
  641.5'39—dc22
                                        2011002450

Editorial Credits
Lori Shores, editor; Juliette Peters, designer; Nathan Gassman,
    art director; Eric Manske, production specialist

Image Credits
USDA/MyPlate.com 4, (MyPlate icon)

Serving sizes are based on recommendations for children ages 4 through 8.

Printed in the United States of America in Stevens Point, Wisconsin.
032011   006240F11

Table of Contents

MyPlate

If you're hungry between meals, a snack can boost your energy.

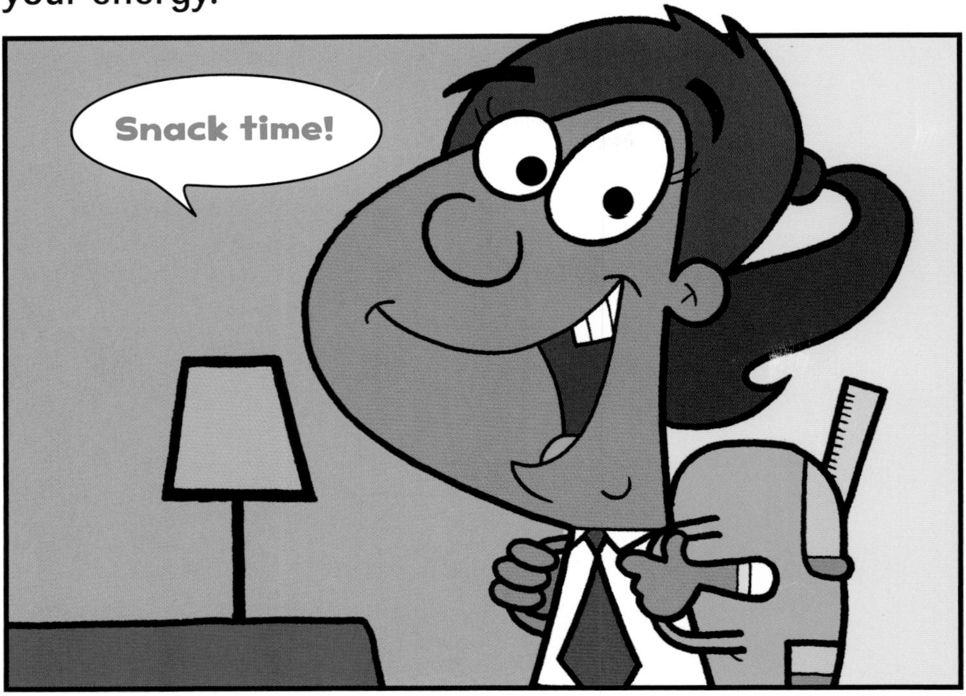
Snack time!

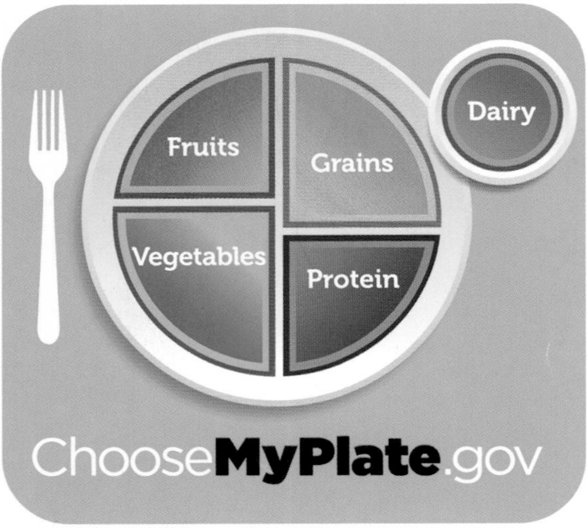
Fruits
Grains
Dairy
Vegetables
Protein
ChooseMyPlate.gov

MyPlate helps you choose healthy snacks. Each colored section stands for a food group.

Your body needs foods from each of the five food groups every day.

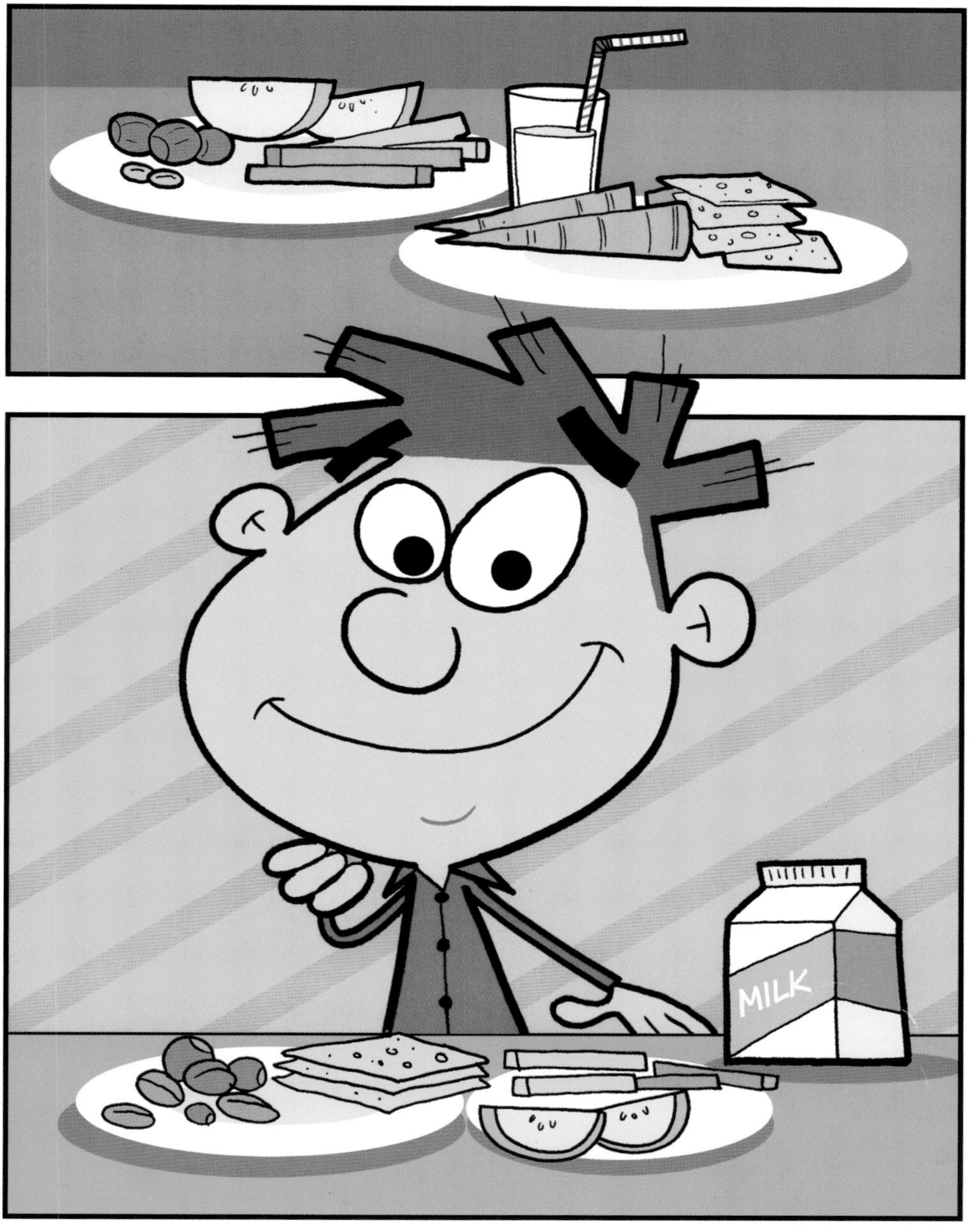
MILK

Snacks help you get all of the servings you need from each food group.

Active kids need food for energy.

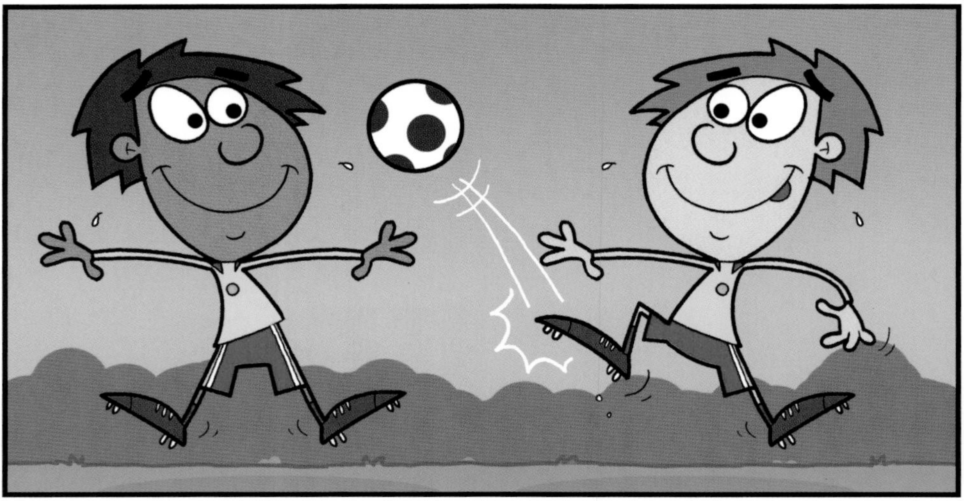

Healthy snacks give you energy to play all day.

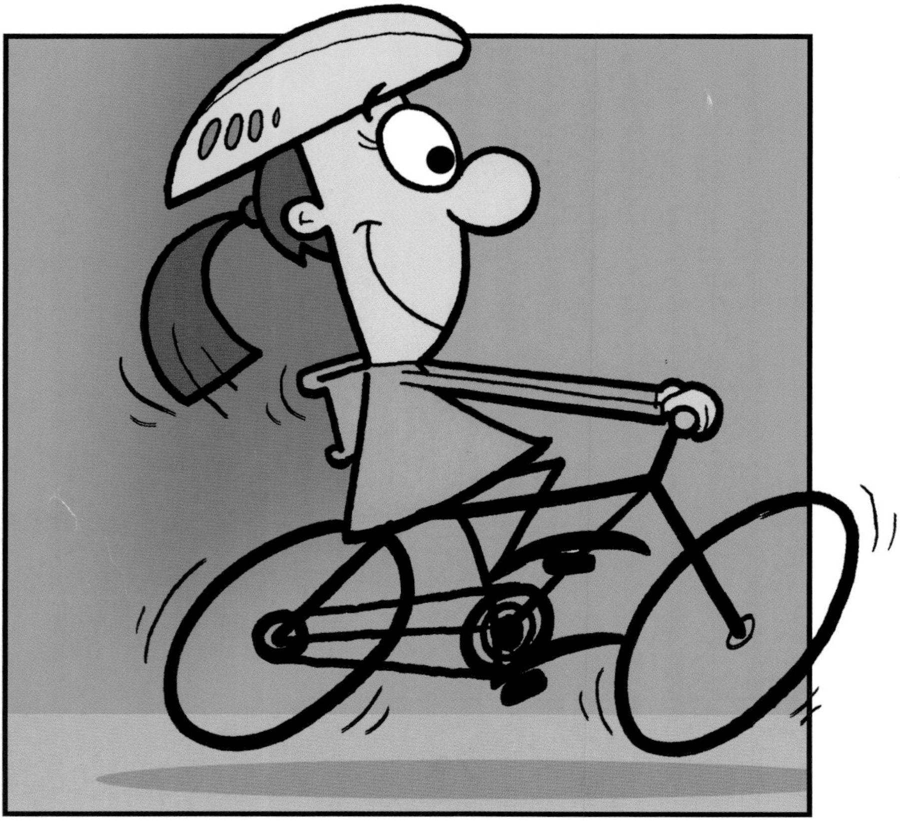

Snacks aren't meals. Snacks should be small.

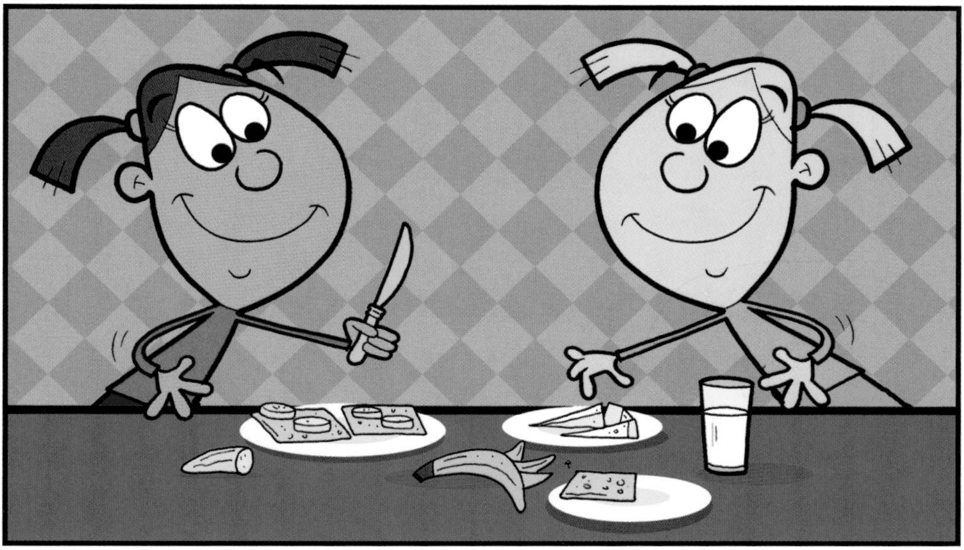

Eating too many snacks will make you less hungry for meals.

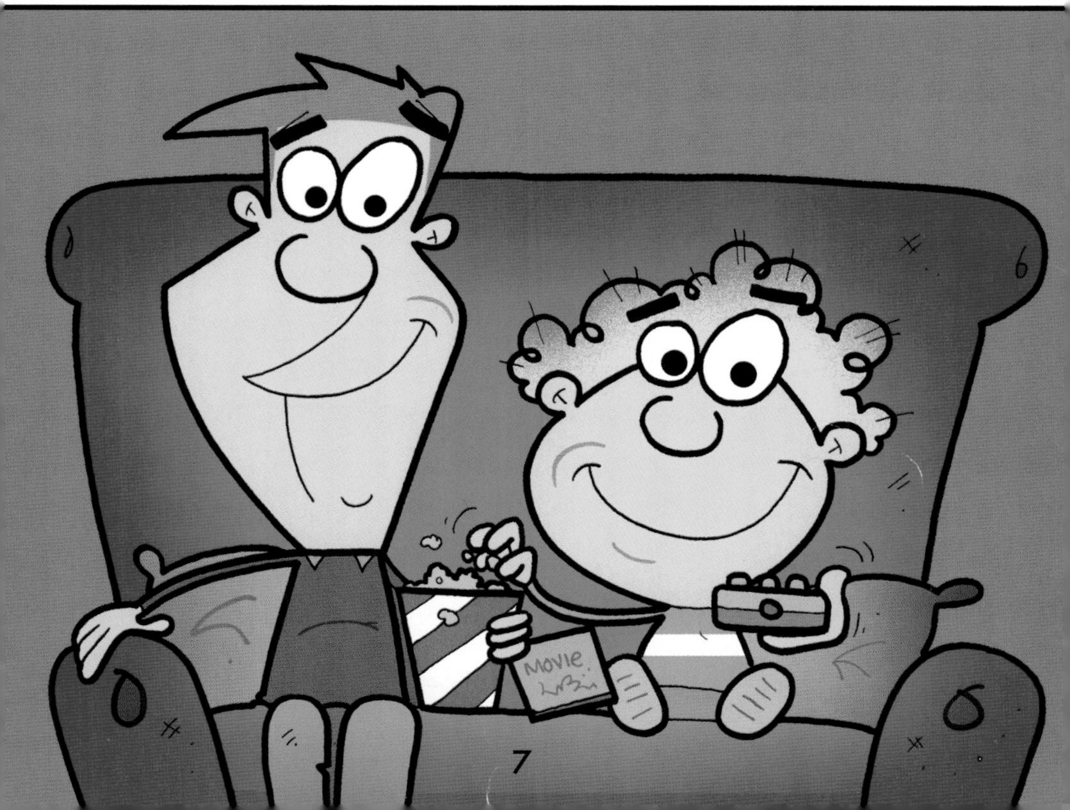
Movie

Snacking with MyPlate

Grains come from wheat and other plants. Some grains are ground into flour to make other foods.

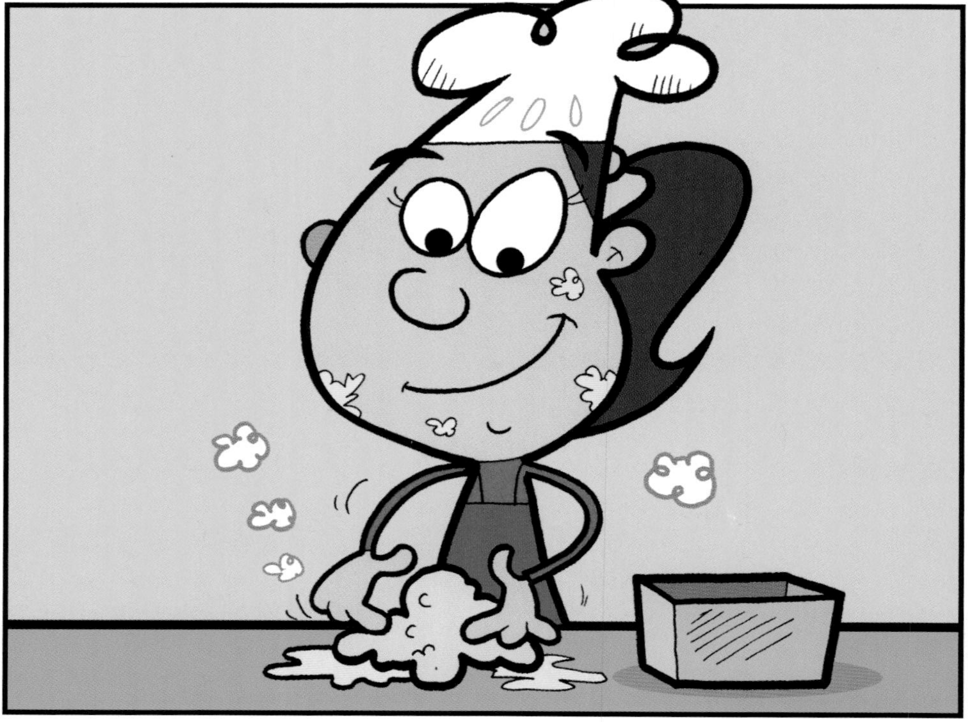

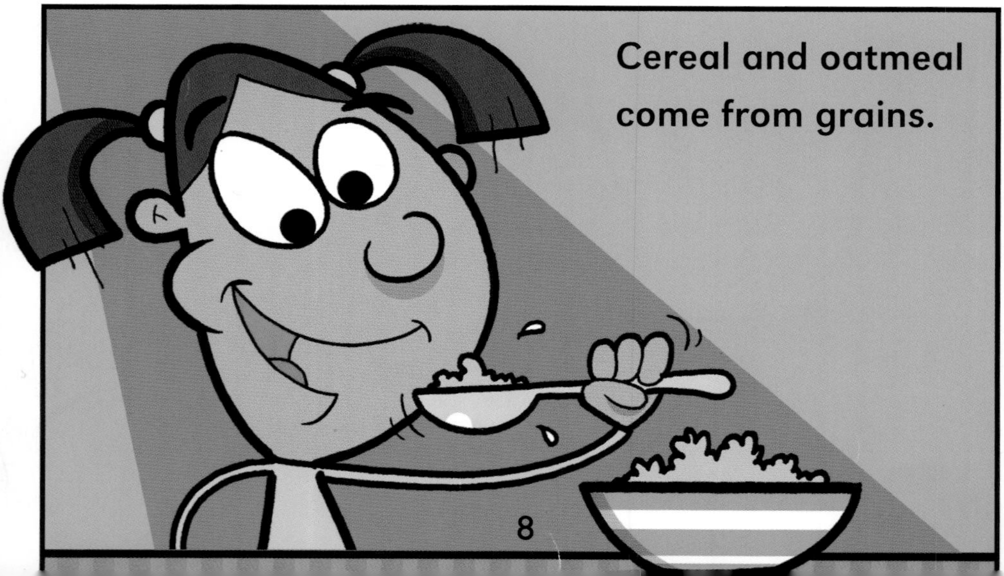
Cereal and oatmeal come from grains.

Whole grain foods have the most nutrients. Half of the grains you eat should be whole grains.

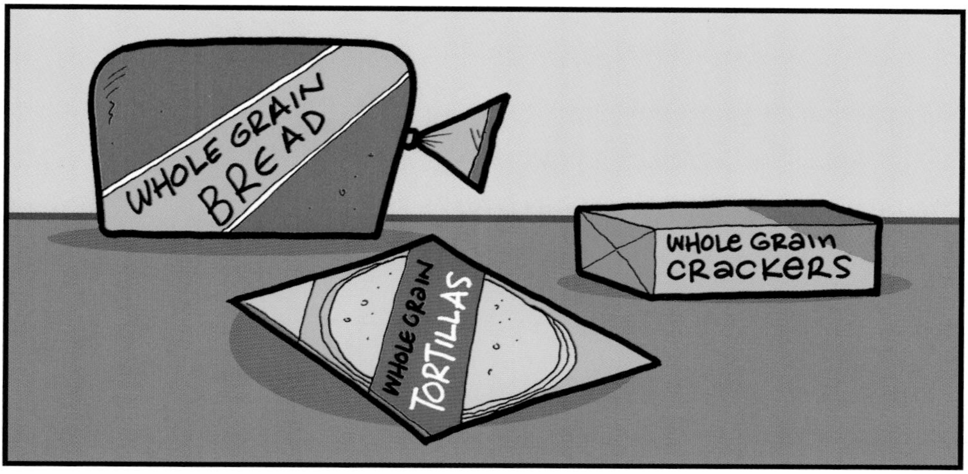
WHOLE GRAIN BREAD
WHOLE GRAIN CRACKERS
WHOLE GRAIN TORTILLAS

Whole grain crackers and rice cakes make good snacks. Add a little cheese or peanut butter to make them more filling.

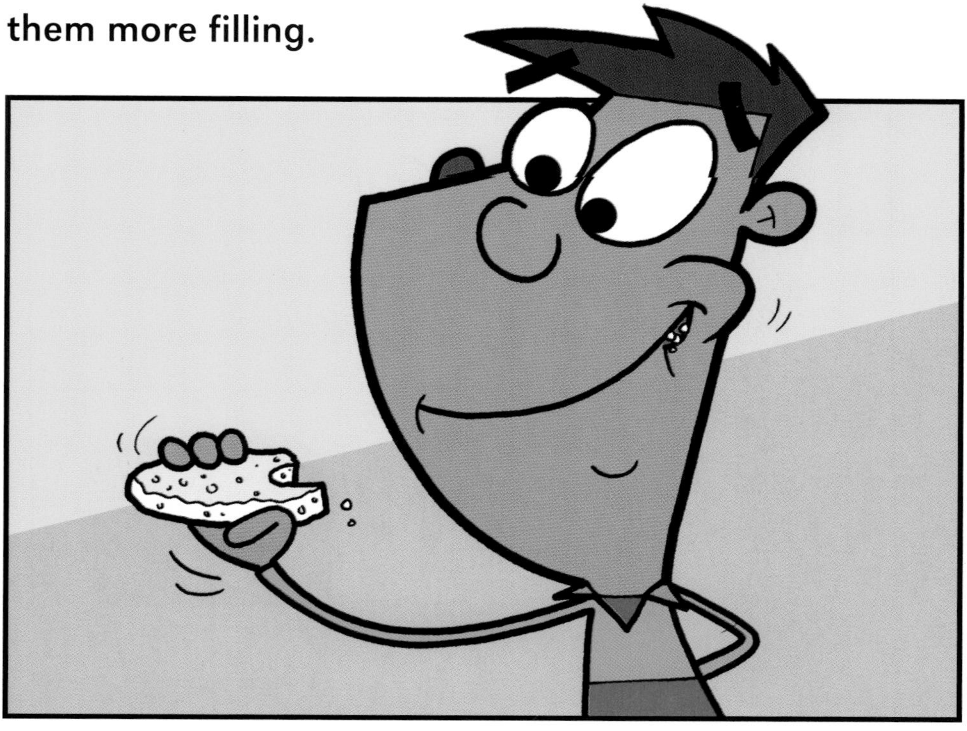

The fruit group gives you fiber and vitamins.

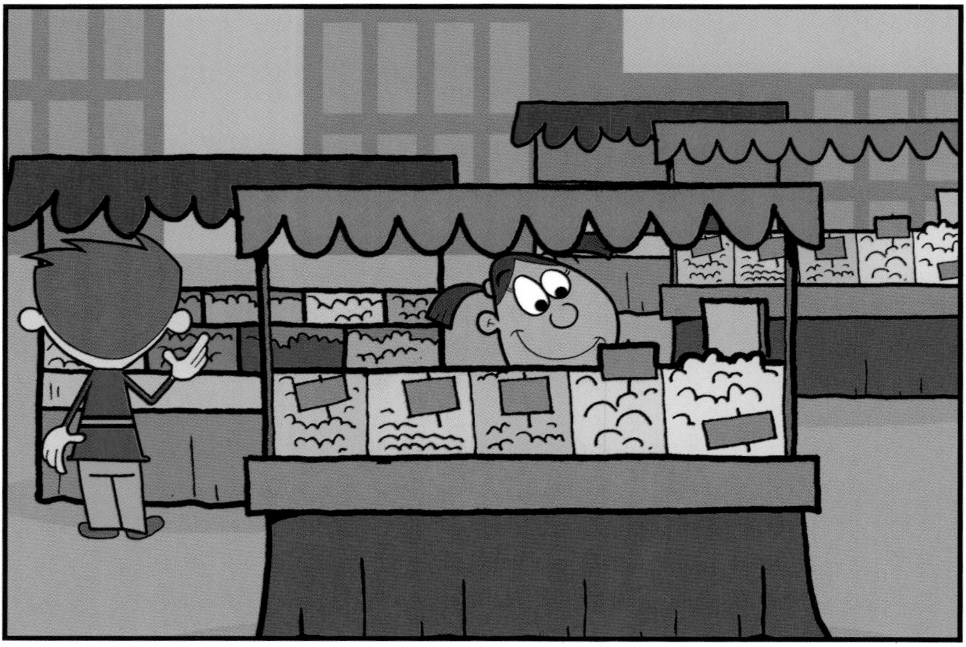

Fruit grows on trees, vines, and bushes.

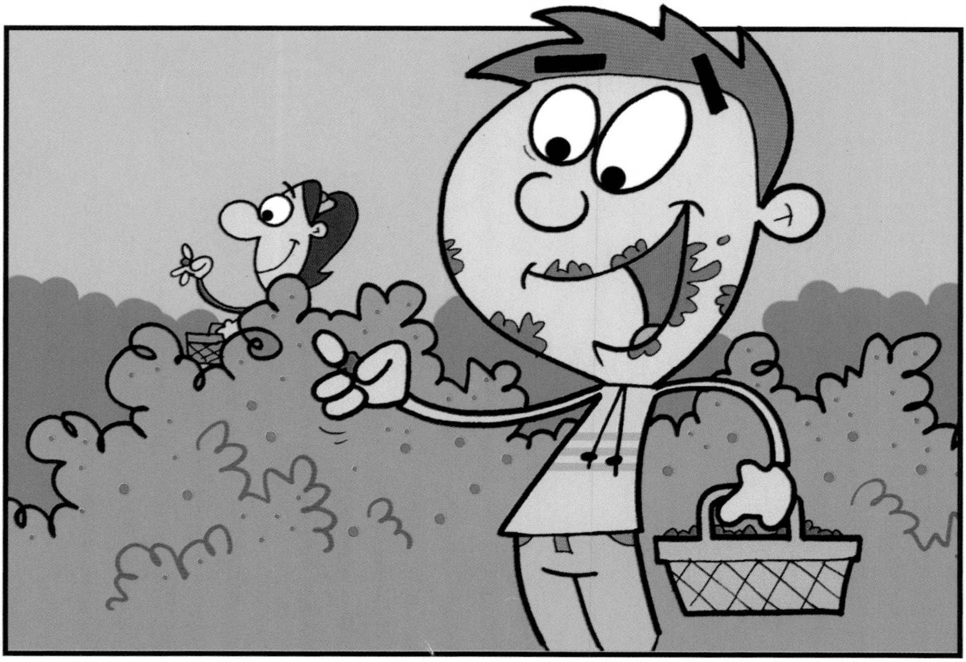

Plums are a juicy snack.

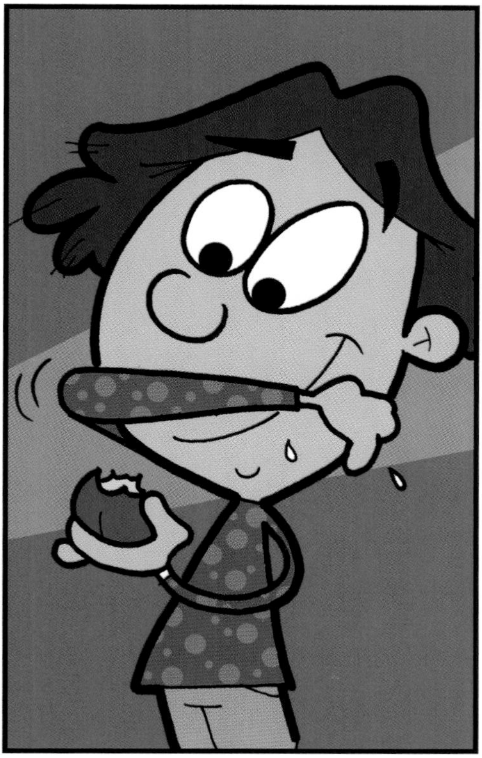

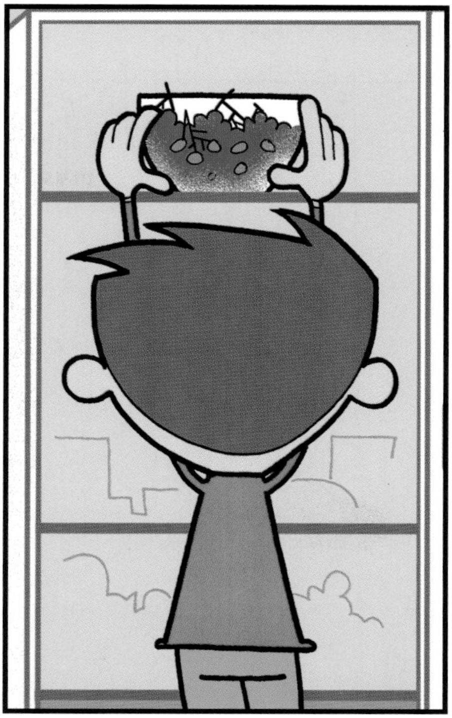

Frozen bananas and grapes make cool treats.

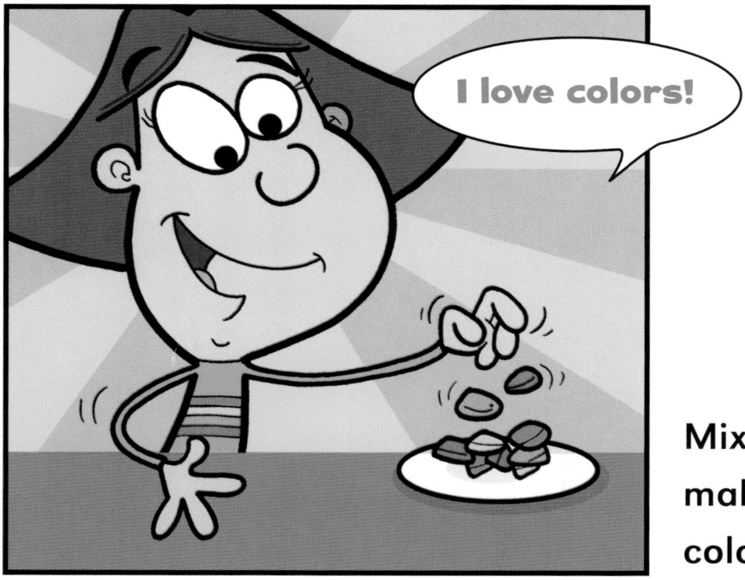
I love colors!

Mixed fruit makes a colorful snack.

Vegetables are packed with nutrients.

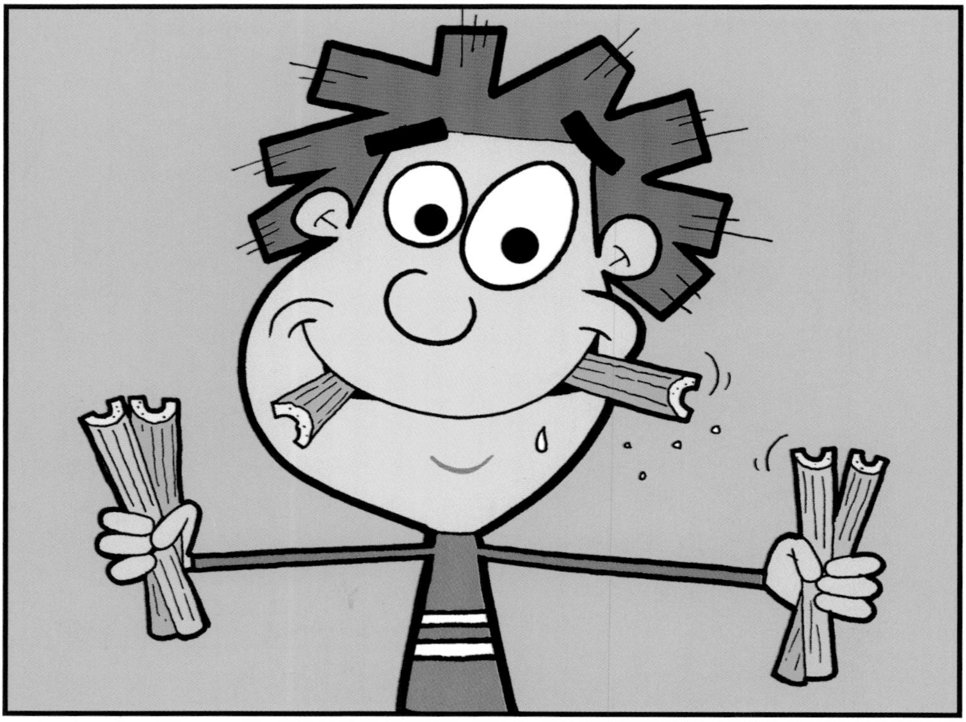

Vegetables grow on farms and in gardens.

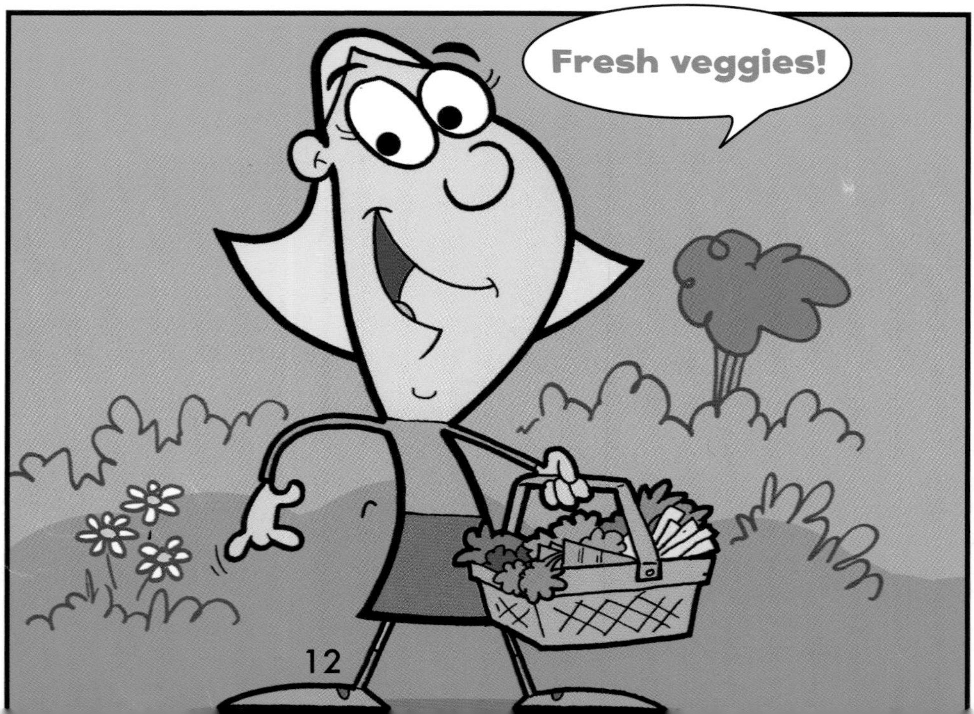
Fresh veggies!

For a snack, dip veggies into low-fat salad dressing.

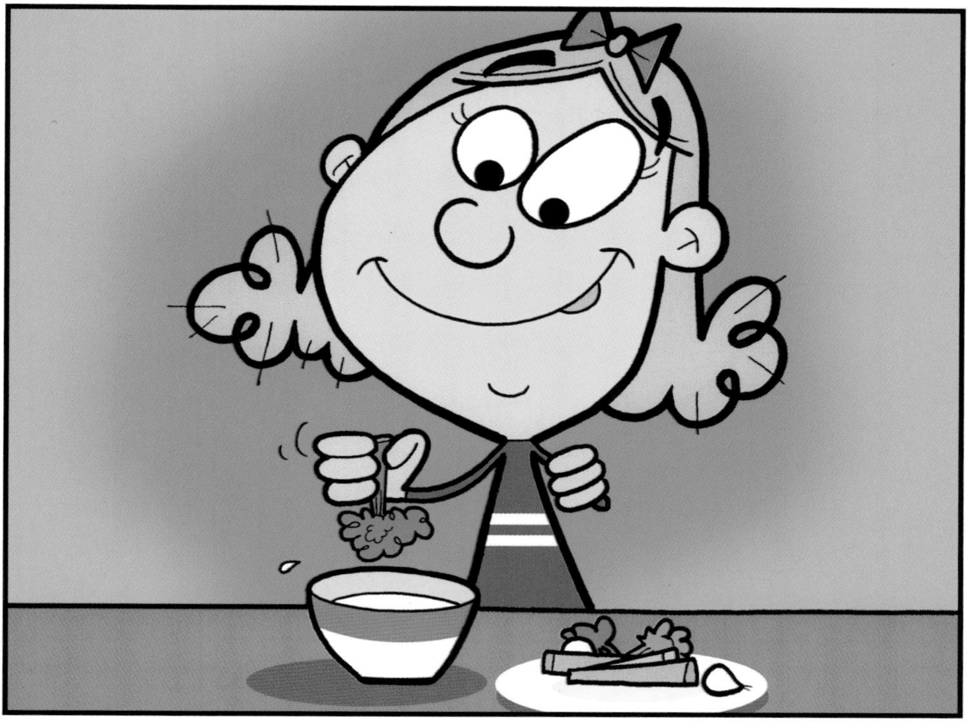

Lettuce, radishes, and cucumbers make a tasty salad.

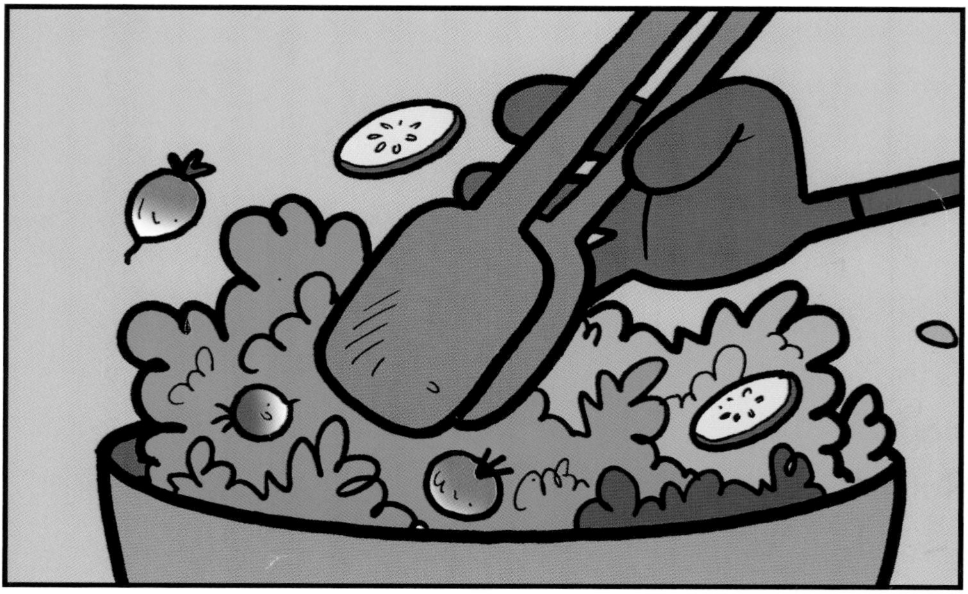

Dairy foods have calcium for strong bones and teeth.

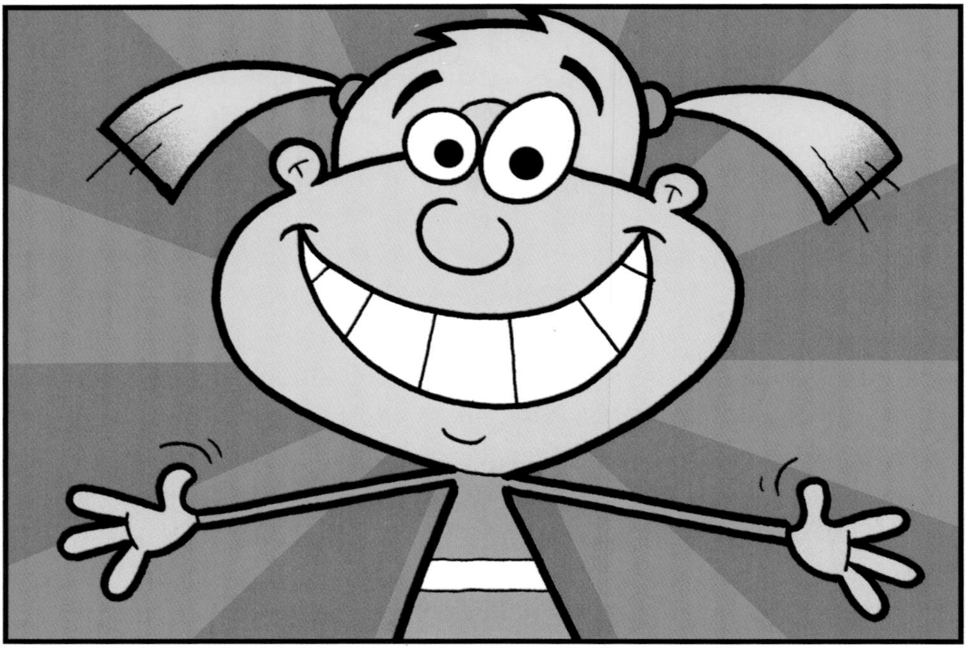

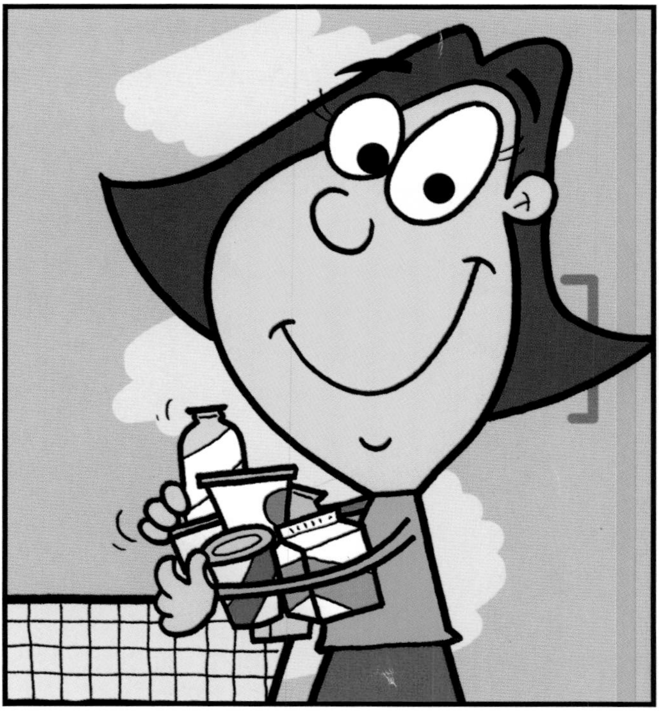

Choose fat-free and low-fat dairy foods for good health.

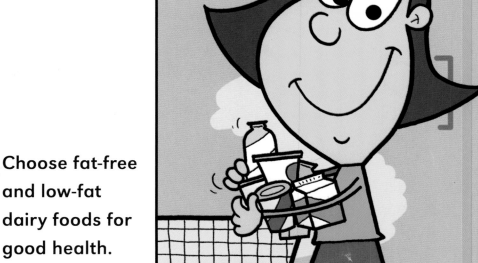

There are many ways to snack on cheese.

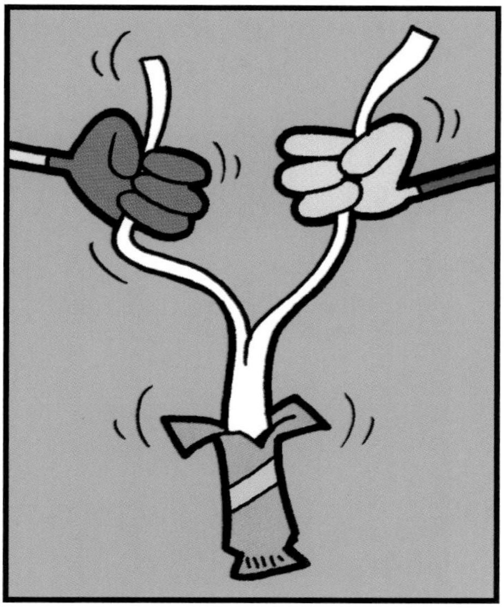

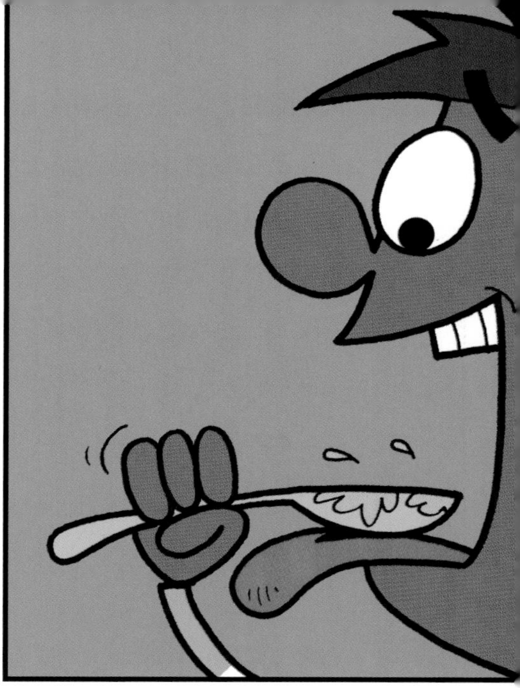

Yogurt is a creamy snack.

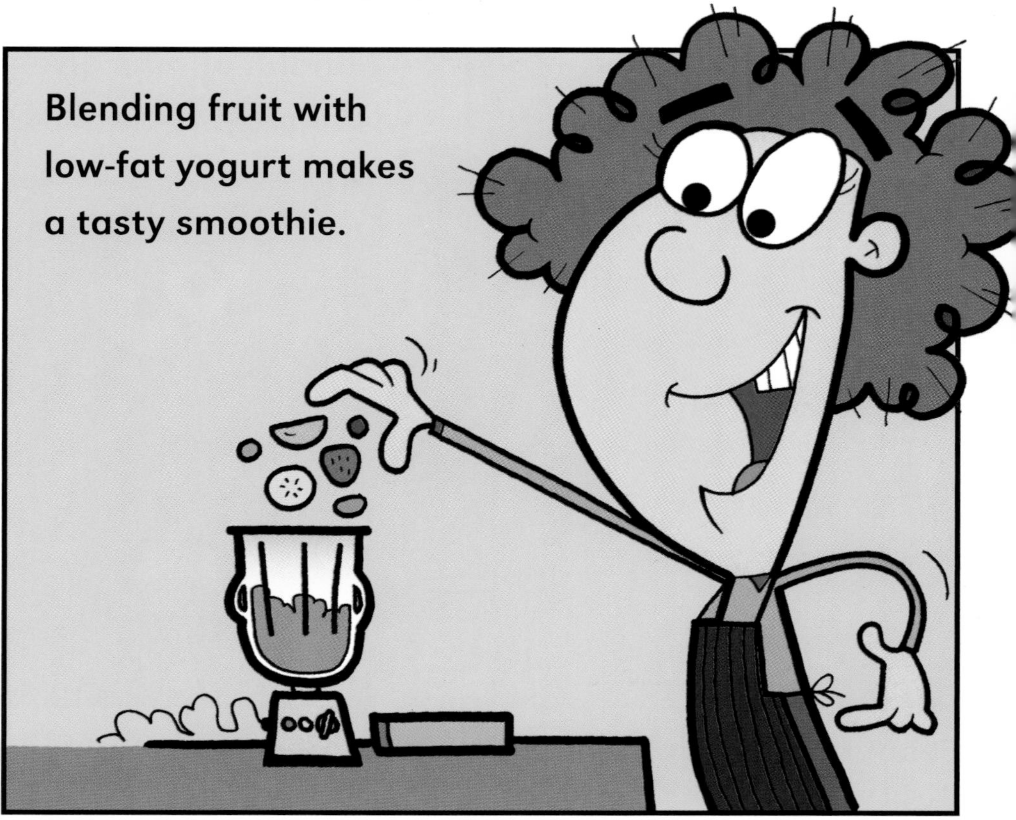
Blending fruit with
low-fat yogurt makes
a tasty smoothie.

Protein foods, such as meat, eggs, and beans, help build strong muscles.

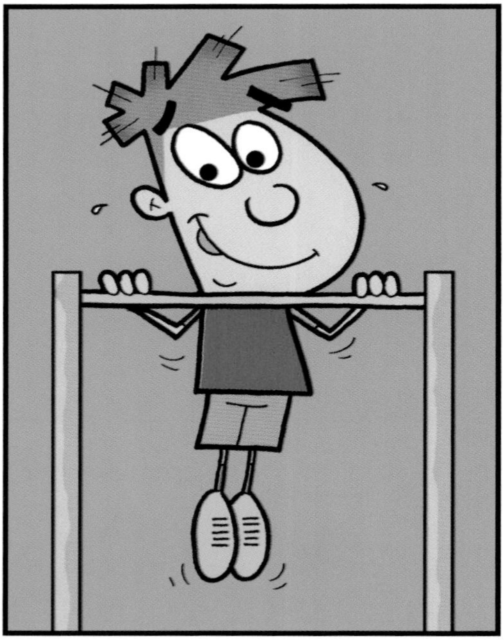

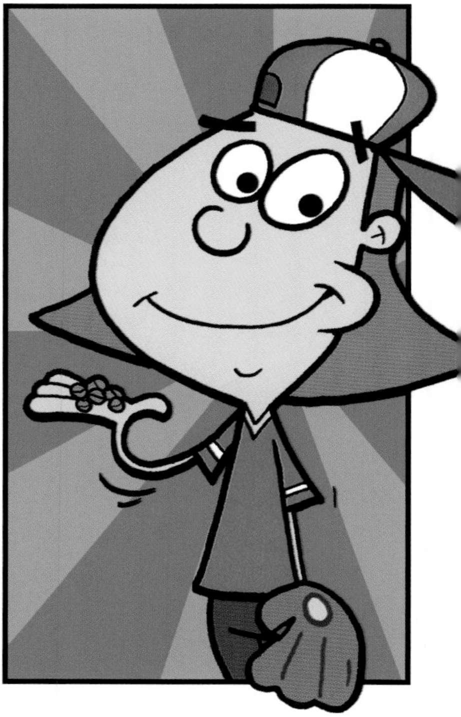

A handful of nuts gives you energy.

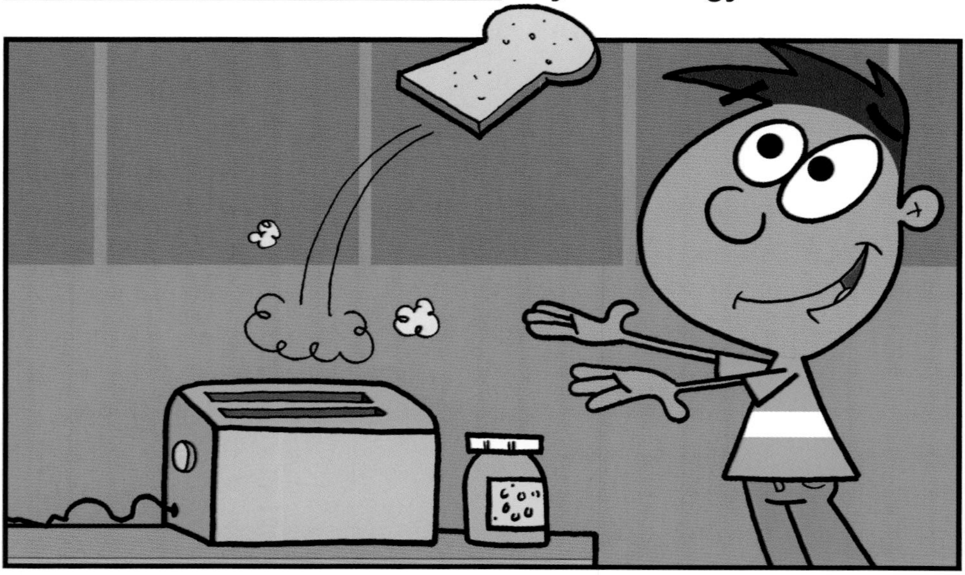

Peanut butter on toast makes a fast snack.

Hummus is made from chickpeas.
It's tasty with veggies!

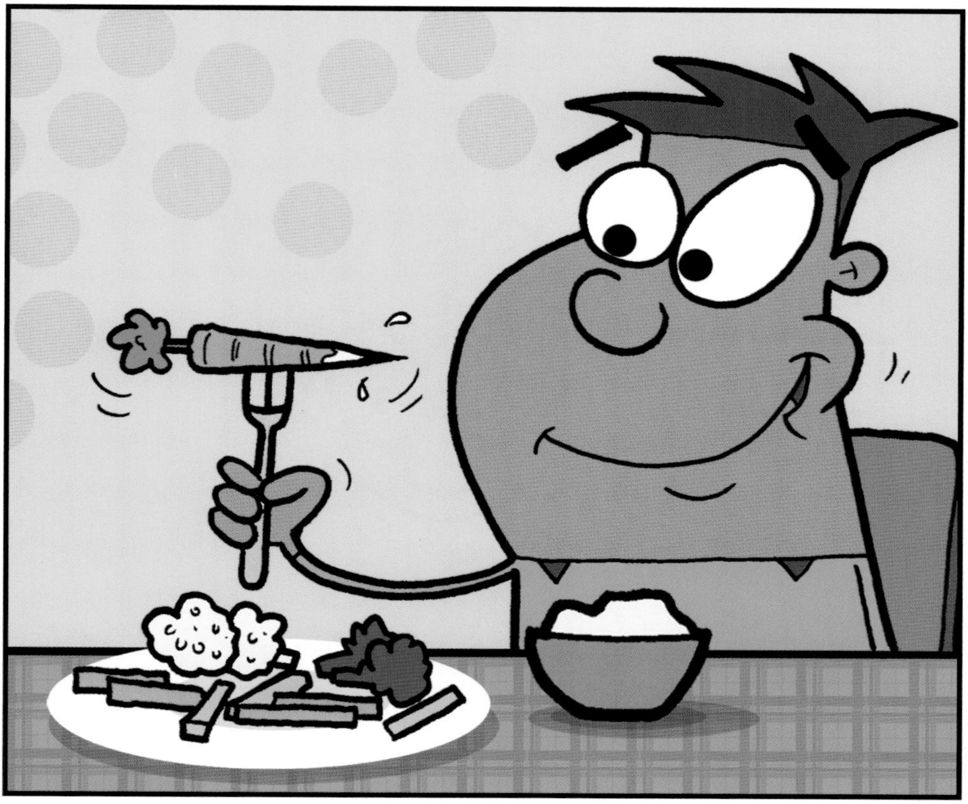

Tuna on whole grain crackers makes a filling snack.

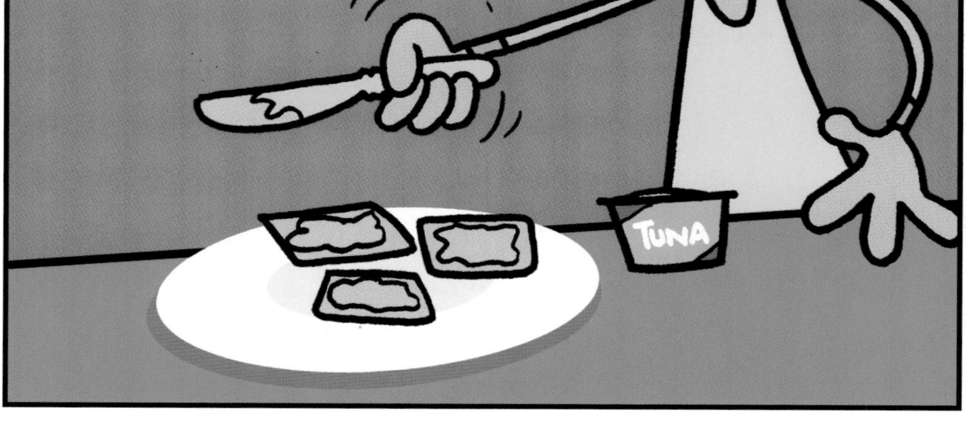
TUNA

Fun with Snacks

What food groups will you choose for your snacks?

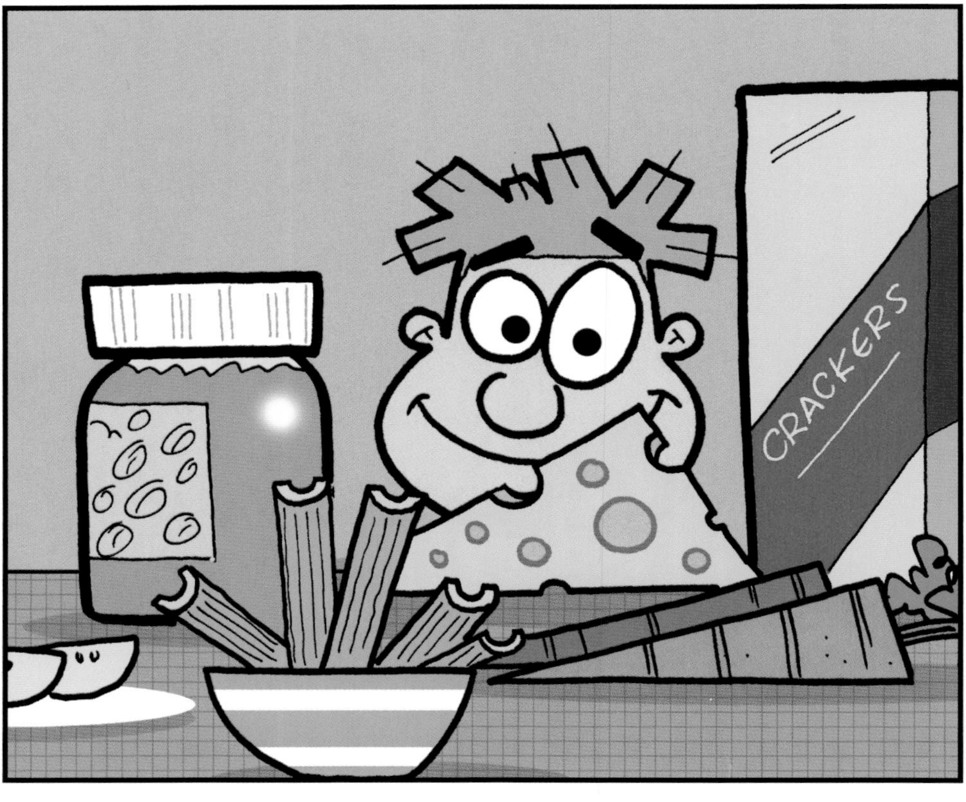
CRACKERS

You can make trail mix with cereal, raisins, and nuts.

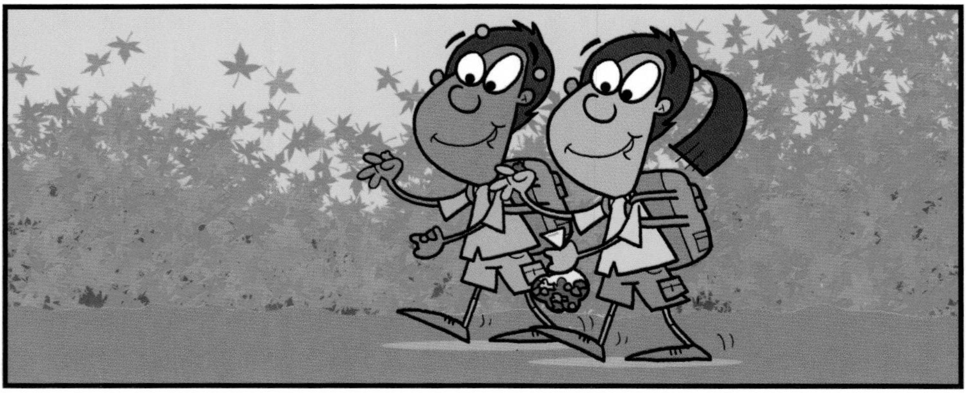

Add fruit and milk to a small serving of cereal.

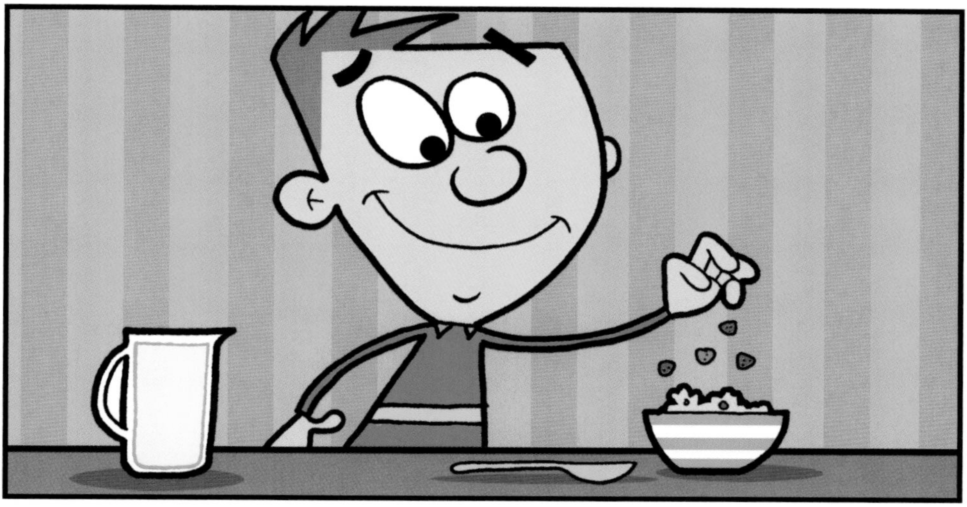

Peanut butter, celery, and raisins make a fun snack.

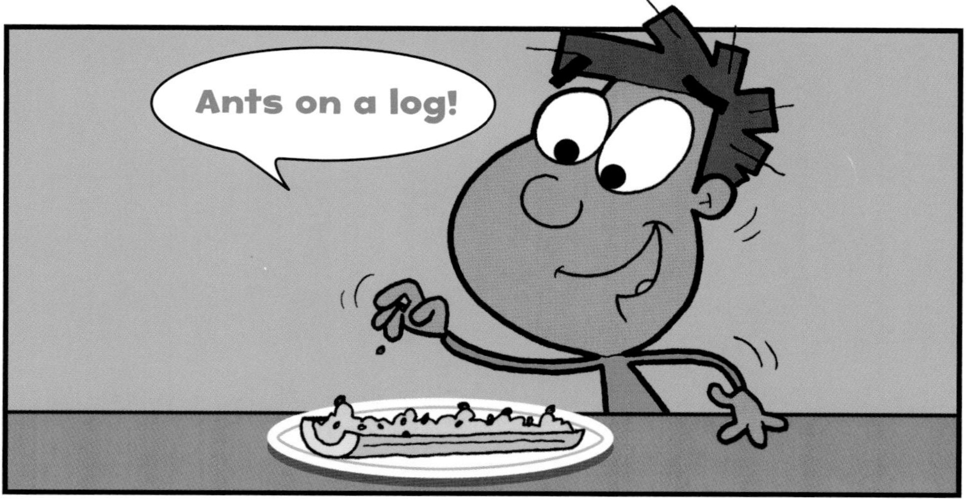
Ants on a log!

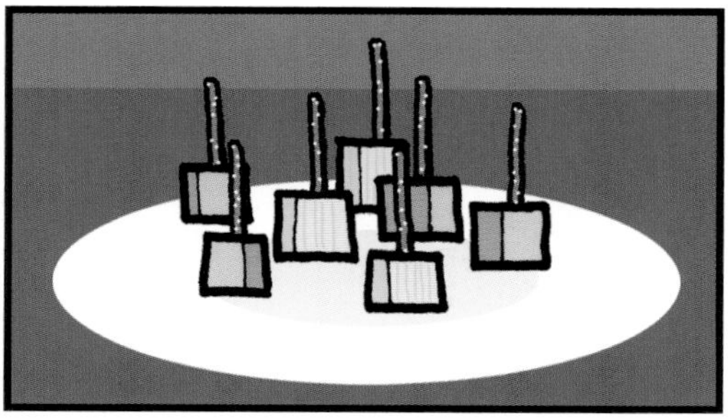

Try putting cheese cubes and pineapple chunks on pretzel sticks.

You can make vegetable faces on mini pizzas.

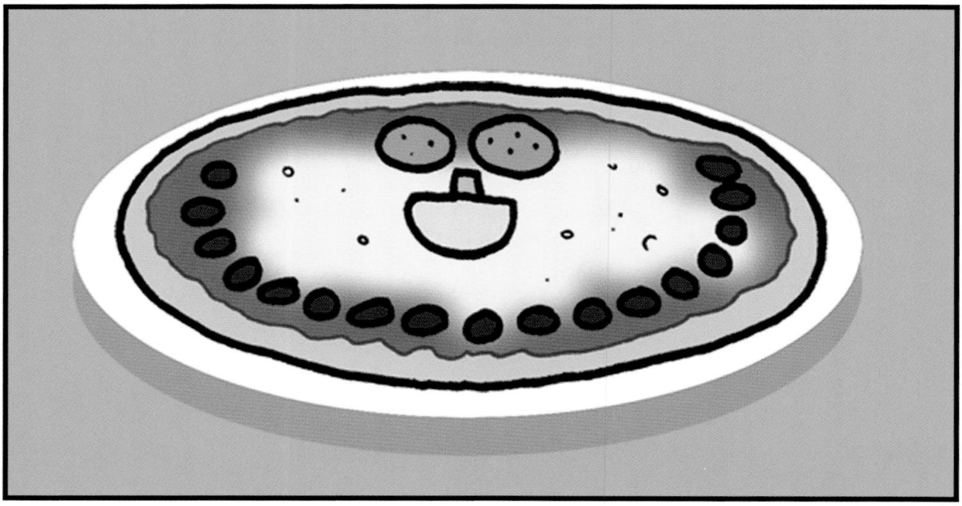

Cheese sails turn hard-boiled eggs into boats.

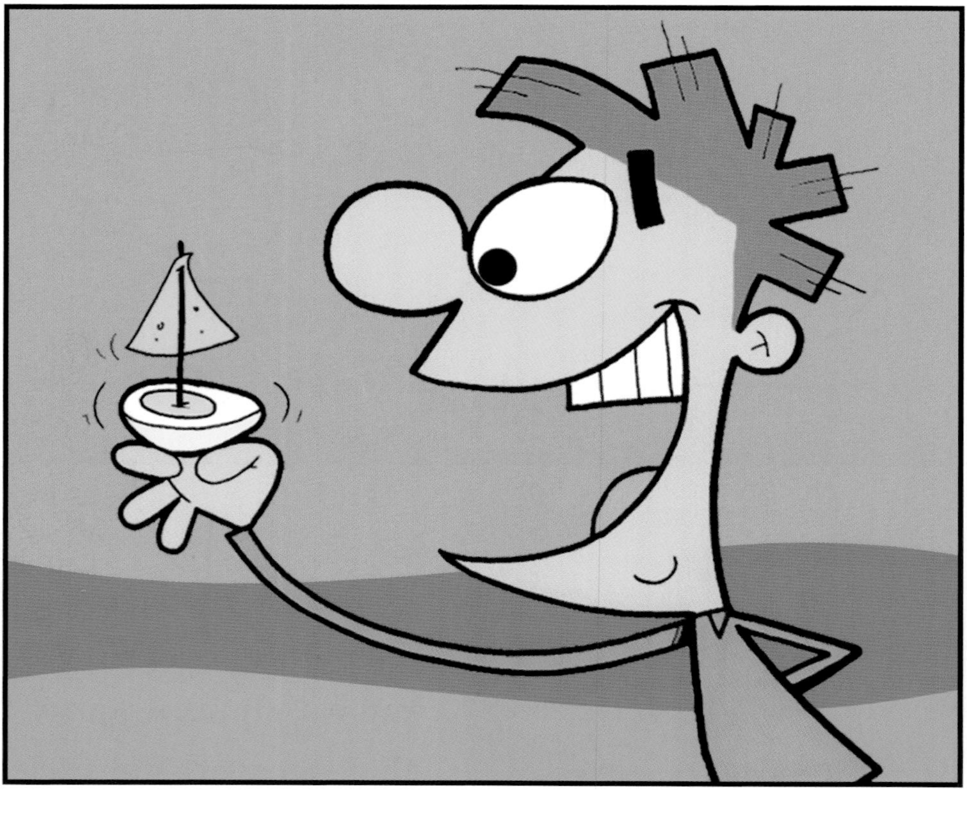

Give strawberry mice some almond ears.

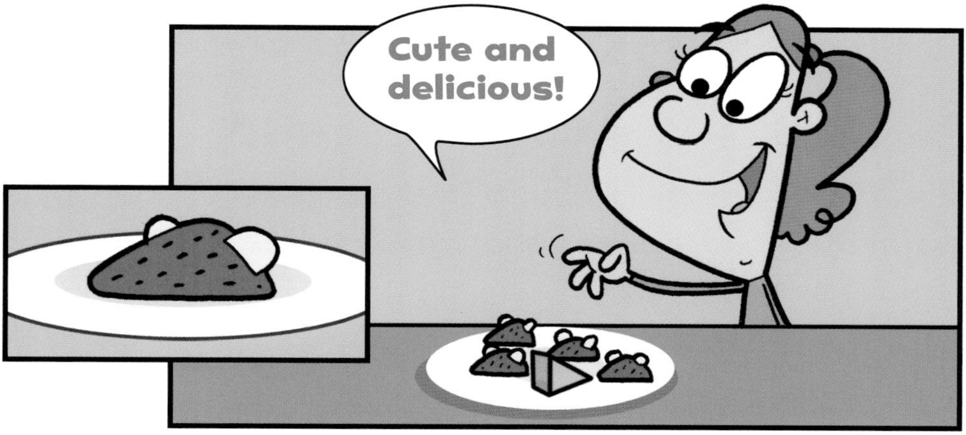
Cute and delicious!

Healthy snacks keep you full of energy.

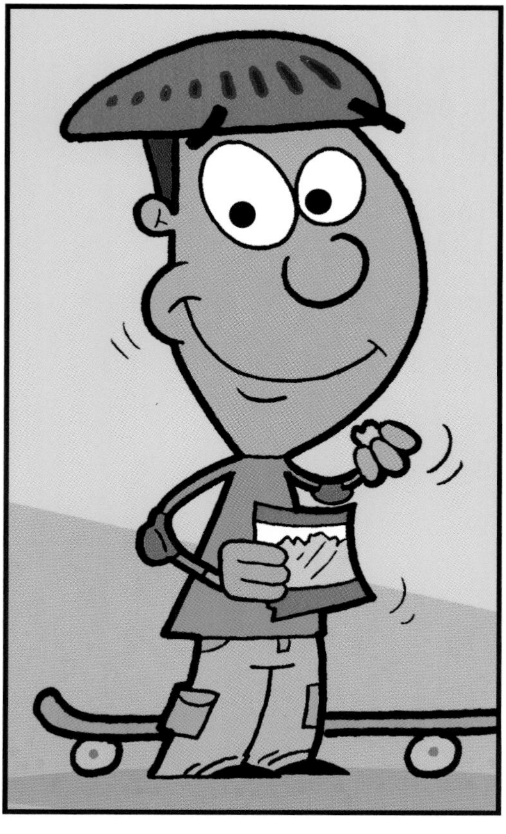

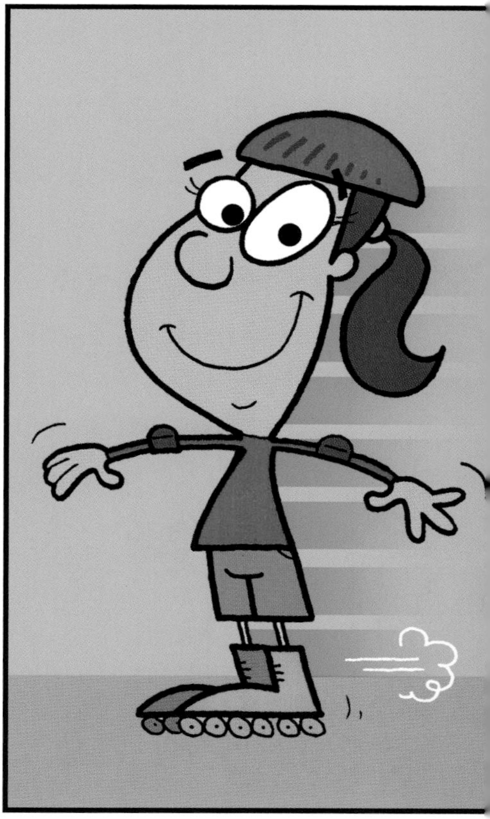

And with more energy, you can have more fun!

Glossary

calcium—a soft, silver-white mineral found in teeth and bones

dairy foods—foods that are made from milk

energy—the strength to do active things without becoming tired

fiber—a part of foods such as bread and fruit that passes through the body but is not digested; fiber helps food move through the intestines

MyPlate—an illustrated guide that explains healthy eating and shows what a balanced meal should look like

nutrient—a substance needed by a living thing to stay healthy; vitamins and minerals are nutrients

protein—a substance found in foods such as meat, cheese, eggs, and fish

vitamin—a nutrient that helps keep people healthy

Read More

Fauchald, Nick. *Holy Guacamole!: And Other Scrumptious Snacks.* Kids Dish. Minneapolis: Picture Window Books, 2008.

Hardyman, Robyn. *Eating Well.* Healthy and Happy. New York: PowerKids Press, 2012.

Malam, John. *Grow Your Own Snack.* Grow It Yourself! Chicago: Heinemann Library, 2012.

Internet Sites

FactHound offers a safe, fun way to find Internet sites related to this book. All of the sites on FactHound have been researched by our staff.

Here's all you do:

Visit *www.facthound.com*

Type in this code: 9781429660938

Super-cool stuff! Check out projects, games and lots more at **www.capstonekids.com**

Index

MyPlate and Healthy Eating

TITLES IN THIS SET:

The Delicious Dairy Group

The Fantastic Fruit Group

The Great Grains Group

Healthy Snacks, Healthy You!

The Incredible Vegetable Group

The Powerful Protein Group

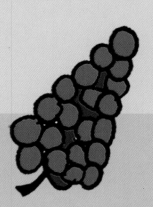
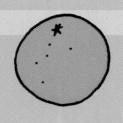